Soapmaking
for the first time ®

To make these opaque bars of soap, refer to the "Here's How" instructions on page 29. Substitute the following liquid colorant combinations and scented oil designations:

Blue: 8 drops blue and 4 drops green; $^{1}/_{4}$ tsp. mint fragrance
Purple: 4 drops red and 2 drops blue; $^{1}/_{4}$ tsp. lavender fragrance
Red/Orange: 5 drops red and 1 drop blue; $^{1}/_{4}$ tsp. raspberry fragrance
Yellow/Orange: 12 drops yellow and 4 drops orange; $^{1}/_{4}$ tsp. citrus blend fragrance

Soapmaking
for the first time®

Linda Orton

Sterling Publishing Co., Inc.
New York
A Sterling / Chapelle Book

Chapelle:

Jo Packham, Owner

Cathy Sexton, Editor

Staff: Areta Bingham, Kass Burchett, Marilyn Goff, Holly Hollingsworth, Susan Jorgensen, Kimberly Maw, Barbara Milburn, Linda Orton, Karmen Quinney, Cindy Stoeckl, Kim Taylor, Sara Toliver, Kristi Torsak

Photography: Kevin Dilley for Hazen Imaging, Inc., and Scot Zimmerman
Gallery Photography: Various professional photographers unknown by name.

If rubber cement is not available in your area, consult any craft store to find a comparable product.

If you have any questions or comments or would like information on specialty products featured in this book, please contact Chapelle, Ltd., Inc., P.O. Box 9252, Ogden, UT 84409 • (801) 621-2777 • (801) 621-2788 Fax • e-mail: chapelle@chapelleltd.com • website: www.chapelleltd.com

To make the transparent bars of soap shown on page 5, refer to the "Here's How" instructions on page 29, substituting white opaque glycerin melt-and-pour soap base for the clear transparent. Refer to the liquid colorant combinations and scented oil designations on page 2.

Library of Congress Cataloging-in-Publication Data Available

10 9 8 7 6 5 4 3 2

Published by Sterling Publishing Company, Inc.
387 Park Avenue South, New York, NY 10016
© 2001 by Linda Orton
Distributed in Canada by Sterling Publishing
c/o Canadian Manda Group, One Atlantic Avenue, Suite 105
Toronto, Ontario, Canada M6K 3E7
Distributed in Great Britain and Europe by Cassell PLC
Wellington House, 125 Strand, London WC2R 0BB, England
Distributed in Australia by Capricorn Link (Australia) Pty Ltd.
P.O. Box 704, Windsor, NSW 2756 Australia
Printed in China
All Rights Reserved

Sterling ISBN 0-8069-6637-8

About the author

Linda Orton lives in the foothills of the Wasatch mountains in Ogden, Utah. She is the mother of five and a grand- mother who enjoys spending time with her family. Linda is married to her best friend, who has always been a terrific supporter through her various "creative stages."

In 1989, she graduated with a B.S. in three-dimensional art and design— with an emphasis in weaving—from Weber State University. Linda has worked in the fields of graphic design and editorial since her graduation.

Linda has always found art and design to be an important part of her life. From childhood on, creativity was encouraged by parents who allowed her to discover her own way. Her interest in fiber arts, particularly in weaving, natu- ral fibers, fabric dyes, and fabric paints, were a stepping stone into the world of scents, herbs, and handmade items, such as handmade soaps, where the creative possibilities are endless.

*This book is dedicated to my family
for their patience and support
when every surface was covered with soap,
as well as to Chapelle, Ltd., and my editor,
Cathy Sexton, for helping to make
one of my passions a tangible reality.*

Table of Contents

Soapmaking for the first time

Introduction

In early times, soapwort root was used for cleansing and Sumerian writings were among the first to contain information about the process of soapmaking. However, early soaps were not used for cleansing the body, but to clean animal skins and prepare them for tanning and hair removal.

One of the first soapmaking factories was preserved in the ruins of Pompeii. Soap for use on the body is believed to have come to the Roman public baths via the Gauls. When the Roman Empire declined, so did personal bathing with soap. It would be several centuries later, in the beginning of the 17th century in England, before bathing with soap would become vogue again.

In the late 1700s, a French chemist by the name of Nicolas Leblanc discovered the process of extracting soda from salt. At the same time, the findings of Louis Pasteur would establish a standard for personal hygiene to reduce the spread of disease, which in turn encouraged bathing with soap.

The early American colonists would make their soap from rainwater that was allowed to run through hardwood ashes to leach out the lye. A raw egg was placed in the lye solution to determine its strength. If the egg dropped to the bottom, the solution needed to be more concentrated and would be run through the ashes again. If the egg floated above the solution, the solution was too strong and needed to be diluted. If the egg floated just beneath the surface, then the lye solution was of the correct concentration. Fat was collected and heated to render the fats suitable for soapmaking. At that time, soapmaking was more of an art than the science it is today, where we have charts and lye calculators that can be used to determine the exact amount of lye and water to be combined with the fats. With the advent of mass production, purchased soap became more economical and was a time-saver for most households.

Handmade soap has been increasing in popularity since the mid 1980s and has gained an even larger following in recent years. The resurgence of soapmaking began primarily in the area of cold-process, which involves the combination of fats and lye solution in a process called saponification. More recently, melt-and-pour soap bases have become the trend since the materials for them can be purchased at the local craft store and need only be melted, colored, scented, and poured into molds. Wherever your interest lies, be it melt-and pour, re-batching, or cold-process, *Soapmaking for the first time* will take you step-by-step through the processes.

Handmade soaps have many benefits for body and mind. Scented oils and botanicals can be added to soap for softening and soothing skin, along with any aromatherapy benefits derived from essential oils. Customize soap to suit your desires in color, fragrance, and/or design. Handmade soaps make unforgettable and personalized gifts for adult and child alike.

How to use this book

For the person who is interested in soap-making for the first time, this book provides a comprehensive guide for the various soapmaking methods. It also provides information on choosing supplies, different techniques, scenting, coloring, and molding. You will learn how different oils and additives are added, not only for aesthetic qualities, but for their beneficial qualities for the skin.

Section 1 will help you familiarize yourself with the basic tools and supplies for the three soapmaking methods that will be taught.

Section 2 contains glycerin melt-and-pour, rebatching, and cold-process techniques and how to add color, fragrance, botanicals, and other visually appealing elements to your hand-made soap. You will learn how to mold bars of soap and loaves that are cut into individual bars.

Section 3 will expand on the previously taught soapmaking techniques and explore the use of more exotic oils, fragrances, and designs. You will learn how to make soap balls on a rope, embed a single shape throughout a loaf of soap, and how to create other personal care items suitable for a gift set.

Section 4 is a gallery of inspiration for any soapmaker—beginner or advanced. Artisans whose soap is as much an art form as it is for practical use are represented in both melt-and-pour and cold-process. A tremendous thanks to all who contributed their products and photographs to show and encourage those who are experiencing soapmaking for the first time.

The primary intent of this book is to teach the basic soapmaking techniques and let you gain the experience and desire to move on and use your creative energies to create and personalize soap for yourself, your family, and your friends.

You may find that you prefer one type of soapmaking over another or that each one has its place in your life because of the distinct benefits and elements of each technique. You will find that you have become pampered and enjoy all the benefits of a handmade soap over those mass-produced. One of the biggest benefits of soapmaking is that you can continue to experiment and create because of its expendable nature.

Section 1:
soap-making basics

What methods are used for soapmaking?

Glycerin Melt-and-Pour

This method is the least technical of the three, yet allows for the most creativity in design. Glycerin melt-and-pour soap base—transparent or opaque—is grated or cut into small squares. The soap base is then melted over medium heat in a double-boiler fashion. A microwave oven can also be used to melt most brands of soap base, but make certain to follow manufacturer's directions when using the microwave. The melted soap base is then poured directly into the prepared mold(s) and allowed to solidify. If the mold that has been used is a loaf-style, it is released from the mold, then cut into individual bars. If individual soap molds have been used, the soap is simply released from the molds. In either case, the soap is ready to be used immediately. Wrapping the finished bars in plastic wrap will help prevent the soap from becoming too dry, in addition to helping preserve the fragrance.

Rebatching

This method of soapmaking involves mixing freshly grated soap with liquid—either water, infused water, or milk. Grated cold-process soap—homemade or purchased—is used. It is then heated on low until the two are blended. The melted soap mixture is then poured directly into the prepared mold and allowed to solidify. Once the soap has been removed from the mold, it is cut into individual bars and allowed to cure.

Cold-processing

This method is the most time-consuming and technical of the three, but the results are worth the extra effort. In this method, a combination of fats (natural oils) are mixed with a lye solution until saponification begins to take place. The soap mixture is then immediately poured directly into the prepared mold and allowed to solidify. Once the soap has been removed from the mold, it is cut into individual bars and allowed to cure.

What can I use as a mold for my soap?

Actual soap molds (shown at left) can be purchased for the purpose of molding soap regardless of the soapmaking method you are using.

In addition, there are many other types of molds available commercially that work great for molding soaps. These include, but are not limited to, candle molds, candy molds, plaster molds, and metal tart shells.

All of the above-mentioned types of molds, which mold individual shapes, work best when using the glycerin melt-and-pour method.

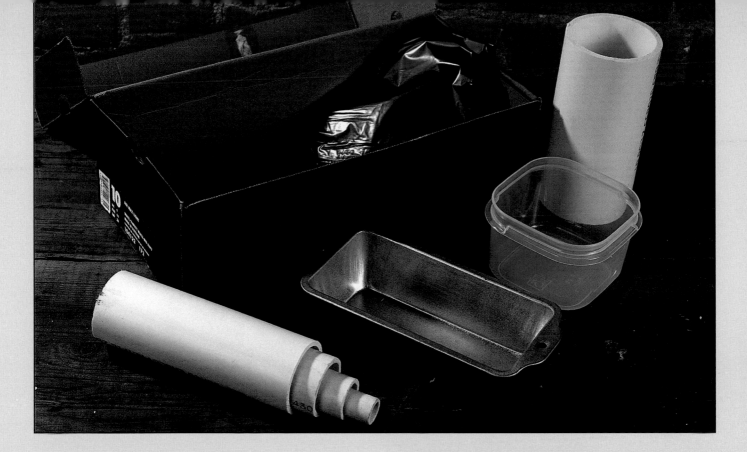

When using an individual mold that has a lot of details and/or intricate designs, you will achieve the best impression if the glycerin melt-and-pour method is used.

Keep in mind that you do not have to purchase any of the previously mentioned types of molds. A number of household items (shown above) can be used as molds for your soap and render wonderful results. Some suggestions include loaf pans, plastic containers, shoe boxes, and plastic PVC® pipe. All of these household items work well for making loaf-style soap—molded in "loaves," then cut into individual bars.

An ordinary shoe box is an exceptional choice as a mold when making cold-process soap. Wooden soap molds with lids are available, but can be expensive.

Regardless of the type of mold you are using, it will need to be prepared prior to the soap being poured into it. When using the glycerin melt-and-pour and rebatching methods, common cooking oil is sprayed into the mold(s). When using the cold-processing method, the mold is lined with a plastic garbage bag.

When using PVC® pipe as a mold, one end must be sealed to prevent the melted soap base from leaking out. Plastic wrap, secured with rubber bands and masking tape, is recommended for sealing the opening.

Important Note:

When choosing a mold to be used for making cold-process soap, use only glass, plastic, stainless steel, or wood—aluminum must not be used because of the reaction between it and the lye in the soap.

What tools and supplies do I need when using the glycerin melt-and-pour method?

Cooking oil spray
Disposable chopstick, bamboo
Glycerin melt-and-pour soap base, transparent or opaque
Heat-resistant glass measuring cup
Kitchen knife, sharp unserrated
Kitchen range or microwave oven
Molds
Skillet, deep

If desired, colorant, scents, botanicals, and other additives can be added.

In addition, metallic or iridescent powders, soap curls, preformed soap shapes, and other small objects, such as seashells, dried flowers, dried fruit, old jewelry, and plastic toys can be added as decorative elements to glycerin melt-and-pour transparent soap.

When using such small objects, caution must be taken to prevent abrasions on the skin. Most importantly, children must be in the company of an adult when using soaps that contain such small objects to prevent choking.

What tools and supplies do I need when using the rebatching method?

Cooking oil spray
Cooling rack
Crockpot or
   Covered casserole dish
Cutting board
Grated soap,
   unscented
Kitchen knife,
   sharp unserrated
Liquid—water,
   infused water,
   or milk
Mold
Oven
Plastic spatula
Wooden spoon

*If desired,
colorant, scents,
botanicals, and
other additives
can be added.*

What tools and supplies do I need when using the cold-processing method?

Bath towels
Blanket
Cooling rack
Cutting board
Disposable chopstick, bamboo
Distilled water
Fats
Glass juice jar with lid
Hammer
Hand blender, optional
Kitchen knife, sharp unserrated
Kitchen range
Laboratory thermometer (with stainless steel shaft), 0° to 180° F
Large nail
Latex gloves
Lye crystals
Measuring cup with pouring spout
Mold, plastic or wooden container with lid
Plastic garbage bag
Protective eyewear
Scale (must be able to weigh up to 5 lb.)
Stainless steel stockpot
Wooden spoon

If desired, colorant, scents, botanicals, and other additives can be added.

What fats can I use when making cold-process soap?

When making cold-process soap, any natural oil can be used. The most commonly used fats include coconut oil, olive oil, and palm oil.

Coconut oil and palm oil both render hard bars of soap with a nice lather. The olive oil is popular for its skin-softening qualities.

Other natural oils—to name a few—that can be used include:

- Almond oil
- Apricot kernel oil
- Jojoba oil
- Shea butter
- Sunflower oil
- Vegetable shortening

What does saponification mean?

Saponification is a chemical process that takes place when a solution made from water and lye crystals is mixed with melted fats. The lye solution and the fats are stirred together and as they become incorporated, the soap mixture thickens until "trace" is reached. The soap mixture is then immediately poured into the prepared mold. Saponification continues for an additional 24 to 48 hours or until the mixture becomes solidified.

Each fat has a saponification value, which measures the amount of lye necessary to saponify one gram of fat. The amounts of the fats, along with their saponification values, are inserted into a mathematical formula that will give the total amount of lye needed to saponify a batch of soap. Saponification charts are available, along with the formula, in advanced soap-making manuals when you become adventurous enough to try some soap formulas of your own.

What does trace mean?

Trace means when the lye solution and fats mixture becomes thick enough that when drizzled from the wooden spoon onto the surface of the remaining mixture in the stockpot, it will leave a visible trail before it disappears.

What do I use to add color to my soap?

Glycerin melt-and-pour soap base can be purchased clear or in a variety of colors, both transparent and opaque. This is the easiest way to add color to soap, but other options are available.

Soap dyes (shown at left) are available in powder, tablet, grated, and liquid forms. Liquid colorant is the easiest of the dyes to use and for that reason is the most popular. It produces intense color so must be used in moderation. Another factor that will determine the intensity of the color is whether it is being used with transparent or white opaque glycerin melt-and-pour soap bases. Keep in mind that the colors will vary greatly when used with rebatching and cold-process soaps. Liquid colorant is available in a limited number of colors, but these basic colors can be mixed to create a myriad of other colors. Food coloring can also be used, but is not as colorfast as liquid colorant.

Herbs and spices can also produce nice color combinations. Typically, one tablespoon to $^1/_4$ cup is added. Some of the most popular herbs and spices that are used include: instant coffee, instant tea, powdered kelp, carotene, liquid chlorophyll, cocoa, cinnamon, curry powder, turmeric, and paprika. Semisweet chocolate can be melted and added for coloration as well.

Natural pigments, also known as inorganic minerals, are available in powder form and render rich hues. These pigments include ochres, iron oxides, ultramarines, and titanium oxides. Make certain you do not breathe in these fine powders when they are being mixed into the soap. Children of any age should not be present when working with pigment powders.

Cosmetic pigments can be used and are typically very highly concentrated colors.

When layering differing colors of glycerin melt-and-pour soap bases, the soap must be thoroughly sprayed with rubbing alcohol (or witch hazel) before each new layer is applied to assure the soap layers bond together and do not separate.

Important Notes:

When adding both color and scent to your soap, always add the colorant before adding the scented oil(s).

When using herbs and spices to add color to soap, the scent of the soap may be altered by the natural scent of the herbs and spices.

What do I use to add scent to my soap?

Scented oils (shown above) are most often used to add scent to soap and fall into two basic categories.

Essential Oils

Essential oils are extracted from plants and are used as a primary scent when making soap. The cost of essential oils varies greatly according to the production costs of extracting the essence—rose one of the most expensive; peppermint one of the least expensive.

Many essential oils have multiple properties and are used for health and aromatherapy benefits. For this reason, only pure essential oils should be used. Make certain they have not been mixed with any base oils.

Fragrance Oils

Fragrance oils are also used as a primary scent when making soap. Fragrance oils are synthetic and imitate popular scents for soaps, lotions, and other body care products.

Fragrance oils are generally less expensive than essential oils and are believed to have less aromatherapy benefits.

Important Notes:

Not all fragrance oils can be used when making cold-process soap.

Potpourri and other oils used for room-scenting should not be used in soapmaking unless stated otherwise by the manufacturer.

Botanicals

Botanicals (shown above) are also used to add scent to soap, but are not ordinarily used as a primary scent. Most often they are used in conjunction with essential or fragrance oils.

Many botanicals are used for the visual appeal they offer and some are used because of the skin-conditioning qualities they possess.

Calendula leaves, chamomile, ground cinnamon, lemon verbena, oatmeal, peppermint, rosebuds, and rosemary are some of the most common botanicals used in soapmaking.

Instant and leaf teas and instant and ground coffees can also be used for scenting soap.

Botanicals may be used whole or ground into smaller particles or powder. The advantage to grinding botanicals is that it allows them to become better incorporated into the soap and to be less irritating to the skin because of a scratchy texture. A coffee grinder, dedicated to grinding spices and botanicals, makes an excellent choice for grinding small amounts of herbs. Food processors and blenders can be used to chop, but usually require a larger amount of herbs than the soap recipe calls for.

What tools and supplies do I need when making a botanical infusion?

Botanical(s)
Distilled water
Glass canning jar
  with lid
Kitchen range
Measuring cup
  with pouring spout
Saucepan
Strainer

What additives with beneficial properties can be used in my soap?

Aloe Vera Gel

Aloe vera gel has a number of skin-nurturing properties and is commonly used in soap.

Clay

Finely powdered French clay (bentonite) and kaolin are added to soap made for oily skin. This soap may be too drying for other skin types.

Honey

Honey has a number of benefits to the skin since it contains enzymes, carbohydrates, B-complex vitamins, and vitamins C and E along with minerals. It also provides a protective film on the surface of the skin that retains moisture.

Oatmeal

Oatmeal is commonly used as a skin exfoliant and skin softener.

Oils

Small amounts of natural oils containing beneficial properties can be added at the end of the soapmaking process. Cocoa butter, shea butter, almond oil, avocado oil, carrot seed oil, and jojoba oil are all popular choices.

Pumice

Ground pumice is a good hand cleanser. The abrasiveness of the soap helps remove dirt and grime.

Section 2: *techniques*

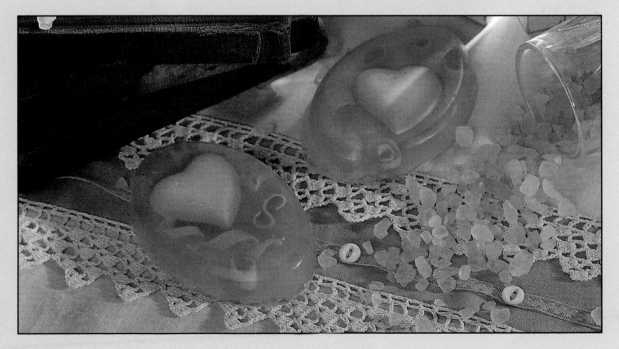

How do I mold and scent glycerin melt-and-pour soap base into decorative bars of soap?

When making decorative bars of soap, using the melt-and-pour method is the easiest. Customized soap can literally be made in a matter of minutes. The glycerin soap base is melted, scented oil is added, then it is poured into molds. Unlike other methods for soapmaking, melt-and-pour soaps are ready for use as soon as the soap cools and sets up.

Glycerin melt-and-pour soap bases are available in transparent (clear and colored) and opaque (white and colored).

What You Need To Get Started:

Cooking oil spray
Disposable chopstick,
  bamboo
Glycerin melt-and-pour
soap base:
  Red transparent, 1 lb.
Heat-resistant glass
  measuring cup
Kitchen knife,
  sharp unserrated
Molds:
  3 Triangles, 4 oz.
Scented oils:
  Cranberry fragrance,
  $^1/_4$ tsp.
  Orange essential,
  $^1/_8$ tsp.
Skillet, deep

Step 2

Cranberry/Orange Jewel Melt-and-Pour Soap Bars

Here's How:

1. Prepare molds by spraying the insides with cooking oil. Wipe away excess oil.

2. Using a sharp kitchen knife, cut the soap base into $^1/_2$" squares and place the squares into a glass measuring cup.

3. Place the glass measuring cup into a deep skillet that has been filled with water.

4. Heat over medium heat until water begins to boil, then immediately reduce heat to low. Using a disposable chopstick, occasionally stir the melting soap base squares.

   Caution: Avoid overstirring to prevent excess bubbles. In addition, overheating will result in a spoiled batch.

Step 4

5. As the melted soap base begins to build-up on the sides of the measuring cup, scrape it back into the measuring cup and allow it to remelt.

6. Remove measuring cup from skillet and allow melted soap base to slightly cool until a "light film" forms on top.

7. Using the chopstick, remove the film and discard.

Step 7

8. Add scented oils to the melted soap base. Using the chopstick, gently stir to evenly distribute the fragrance.

   Caution: Make certain to mix thoroughly to avoid oil pockets from forming on the bottom of the bars of soap, but avoid overstirring or stirring briskly to prevent excess bubbles.

Step 8

9. Pour the melted soap base into prepared molds and allow to cool until solidified.

   Note: To reserve for use at a later time, excess soap base can be poured into a plastic storage container that has been sprayed with cooking oil.

10. Turn the molds over and release the bars of soap.

    Note: Filled molds may be placed in the refrigerator to speed the cooling process. If the soap does not release from the mold, place mold in the freezer for approximately 10 minutes. Remove mold from freezer and allow to sit until condensation forms. Soap should then easily release from mold.

Step 9

Step 10

Design Tip: If colored glycerin melt-and-pour soap base is not available, a colorant can be added to the soap base. See Technique 2 on pages 28–29.

To make the opaque bars of soap, refer to the "Here's How" instructions on the following page, substituting white opaque glycerin melt-and-pour soap base for the clear transparent.

How do I add color to glycerin melt-and-pour soap base to make colorful bars of soap?

Colorant comes in powder, tablet, grated, and liquid forms. Liquid colorant is the easiest to use and is available in red, yellow, blue, green, and orange. These basic colors are mixed to create other colors. Liquid colorant should be used in moderation as the colors can be intense. In addition, the colorant will vary depending on whether it is used with transparent or white opaque glycerin melt-and-pour soap base.

What You Need To Get Started:

Cooking oil spray
Disposable chopstick, bamboo
Glycerin melt-and-pour soap base:
  Clear transparent, $^1/_2$ lb.
Heat-resistant glass measuring cup
Kitchen knife, sharp unserrated
Liquid colorants:
  Blue
  Yellow
Molds:
  2 Ovals, 4 oz.
Scented oils:
  Sage fragrance, $^1/_8$ tsp.
  Sweetgrass fragrance, $^1/_8$ tsp.
Skillet, deep

See pages 1 and 5 for additional photos of bars of soap using this technique. Liquid colorant combinations and scented oil designations are provided.

Step 2

Spirit-of-the-Earth Melt-and-Pour Soap Bars

Here's How:

1. Refer back to Technique 1: Steps 1–7 on pages 25–26.

2. Add one drop blue and nine drops yellow liquid colorant to the melted soap base. Using the chopstick, gently stir to evenly distribute the color.

3. Refer back to Technique 1: Steps 8–10 on pages 26–27.

Design Tip: If using powder colorant, use minute amounts to achieve desired colors as this type of colorant renders the most intense colors. If using solid colorant, slivers are cut from the block and added to the soap base during the melting process.

How do I mix two colors of glycerin melt-and-pour soap base to make swirled bars of soap?

Swirled soaps are not only attractive to look at, but they also allow for a blending of complementary fragrances. A lovely, swirled soap is created by gently mixing two or more colors of soap together. In this case, the combination of almond and coffee bean fragrances create a lovely amaretto scent.

3
technique

What You Need To Get Started:

Butter knife
Cooking oil spray
Disposable chopstick,
   bamboo
Glycerin melt-and-pour
soap base:
   White opaque, 1^1/$_2$ lb.
2 Heat-resistant glass
   measuring cups
Instant coffee, 2 tbsp.
Kitchen knife,
   sharp unserrated
Mold:
   Small loaf pan,
   6^1/$_2$" long x
   3" wide x 2" deep
Scented oils:
   Almond fragrance,
      ^{3}/$_8$ tsp.
   Coffee bean fragrance,
      ^{1}/$_4$ tsp.
Skillet, deep

Swirled Almond/Coffee Bean Melt-and-Pour Soap Bars

Here's How:

1. Refer back to Technique 1: Steps 1–5 on pages 25–26.

2. Pour one-quarter of the melted soap base into a clean glass measuring cup and set to one side in the deep skillet.

3. Refer back to Technique 1: Steps 6–8 on page 26, adding only the almond frag-rance scented oil to the melted soap base.

4. Pour the melted soap base (almond) into prepared mold.

5. Add coffee bean fragrance scented oil to the reserved melted soap base. Using the chopstick, gently stir to evenly distribute the fragrance.

6. Add the instant coffee to the melted soap base (coffee bean). Using the chopstick, gently stir to evenly distribute the color.

7. Pour the melted soap base (coffee bean) into prepared mold on top of the almond layer.

8. Using a butter knife, gently "cut through" the two soap mixtures enabling the colors to "swirl" together and allow to cool until solidified.

    Caution: Avoid overmixing or soap will not render a swirled effect.

9. Refer back to Technique 1: Step 10 on page 27.

10. Using the sharp kitchen knife, slice the soap into individual bars.

    Note: The two soap mixtures can be "swirled" together in individual molds, but care must be taken to avoid overmixing.

Step 8

Design Tips:

Another method of "swirling" two colors of soap base is to simultaneously pour both soap mixtures into the pre-pared mold(s).

Melt one ounce of semisweet choco-late and mix into reserved soap base in place of coffee bean fragrance and instant coffee in Steps 5 and 6 above.

Substitute vanilla fragrance for the almond fragrance. Then add cinnamon essential oil and one tablespoon cinna-mon powder into reserved soap base in place of coffee bean fragrance and instant coffee in Steps 5 and 6 above.

4
technique

**What You Need
To Get Started:**

Cooking oil spray
Disposable chopstick,
  bamboo
Glycerin melt-and-pour
soap base:
  Yellow opaque, ¼ lb.
Heat-resistant glass
  measuring cup
Kitchen knife,
  sharp unserrated
Mold:
  Three-dimensional
  rubber duck
Paper towels
Paring knife
Scented oil:
  Sunflower fragrance,
  ⅛ tsp.
Skillet, deep

How do I mold glycerin melt-and-pour soap base into three-dimensional bars of soap?

Three-dimensional rubber duck soap is perfect for a child's bathroom. Dimensional molds are available in other shapes as well, such as seashells. This dimensional soap is prepared in a mold that snaps together and has a pour spout on top.

Three-dimensional Rubber Duck Melt-and-Pour Soap Bars

Here's How:

1. Refer back to Technique 1: Steps 1–8 on pages 25–26.

2. Pour the melted soap base into prepared mold through the hole at the top of the mold and allow to cool until solidified.

3. Gently pull the mold apart to release the three-dimensional bar of soap.

4. Using a paring knife, trim away the excess soap that has been molded to the bar.

   Note: After trimming the soap, the ridge can be smoothed further by dampening your finger and rubbing it along the ridge. Gently rub the dampened ridge with a paper towel.

Step 2a

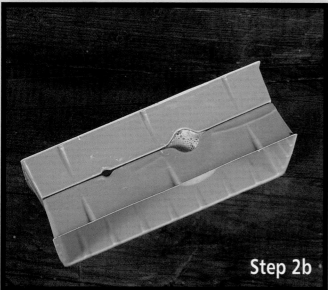

Step 2b

Step 4

Design Tip: Three-dimensional candle and/or plaster molds also can be used as molds in soapmaking.

How do I mold glycerin melt-and-pour soap base into layered bars of soap?

Layered bars of soap have more aesthetic value than anything else. However, layering also allows for complementary fragrances to be combined within each individual layer. The inspiration for this soap was a favorite ice cream flavor.

Orange Crème Melt-and-Pour Soap Bars-on-a-Stick

Here's How:

1. Refer back to Technique 1: Steps 1–7 on pages 25–26, using only 1/2 lb. of the white opaque soap base.

2. Refer back to Technique 1: Step 8 on page 26, adding 1/8 tsp. vanilla fragrance scented oil to the melted soap base.

3. Refer back to Technique 1: Step 9 on page 27, filling the prepared mold no more than one-third full.

4. Refer back to Technique 1: Steps 1–7, using the clear transparent soap base.

5. Refer back to Technique 2: Step 2 on page 29, adding two to four drops orange liquid colorant to the melted soap base.

6. Refer back to Technique 1: Step 8, adding orange essential scented oil to the melted soap base.

7. Spray a light mist of rubbing alcohol on top of the vanilla layer.

   Note: Make certain to coat the layer of soap evenly to assure the soap layers bond together and do not separate.

8. Refer back to Technique 1: Step 9, pouring the orange melted soap base onto the vanilla layer.

   Note: The prepared mold should be no more than two-thirds full.

9. Refer back to Technique 1: Steps 1–7, using the remaining 1/2 lb. of the white opaque soap base.

What You Need To Get Started:

Cooking oil spray
4 Craft sticks
Disposable chopstick, bamboo
Glycerin melt-and-pour soap bases:
    Clear transparent, 1/2 lb.
    White opaque, 1 lb.
2 Heat-resistant glass measuring cups
Kitchen knife, sharp unserrated
Liquid colorant:
    Orange
Mold:
    Desk organizer, 18" long x 2 3/4" wide x 2" deep
Rubbing alcohol
Scented oils:
    Orange essential, 1/8 tsp.
    Vanilla fragrance, 1/4 tsp.
Skillet, deep
Spray bottle

10. Refer back to Technique 1: Step 8, adding $\frac{1}{8}$ tsp. vanilla fragrance scented oil to the melted soap base.

11. Spray a light mist of rubbing alcohol on top of the orange layer.

Step 11

12. Refer back to Technique 1: Step 9, pouring the vanilla melted soap base onto the orange layer.

    Note: The prepared mold should be full to within $\frac{1}{2}$" from the top.

13. Refer back to Technique 1: Step 10 on page 27.

14. Using the sharp kitchen knife, cut the bar of soap into four equal lengths.

15. Spray a light mist of rubbing alcohol onto each craft stick and gently push into the middle (orange) layer at one end of each bar of soap to resemble an ice cream bar.

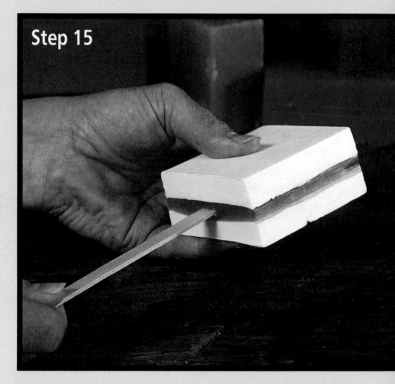

Step 15

Design Tip: A blended effect can be achieved by allowing a thick film to form on each layer, then pouring a new layer before the previous layer has set-up.

What You Need To Get Started:

Cutting board
Rubber mallet or
   hammer
Soap bars:
   Molded glycerin
   melt-and-pour or
   freshly cut
   cold-process
Soap stamp,
   rubber stamp, or
   sealing wax stamp

Stamped Soap Bars

Here's How:

1. Place the bars of soap onto a large cutting board that has been dedicated to soap-making.

2. Place the stamp on the surface of the soap as desired.

3. Using a rubber mallet, strike the top of the stamp four to six times. Judge your strikes according to the hardness of the soap bar.

How do I make stamped impressions on bars of soap?

Soap stamps, rubber stamps, and sealing wax stamps with large details can be used to make stamped impressions on bars of soap. Generally glycerin melt-and-pour bars of soap can be stamped any time, but the best impressions are made after unmolding if the soap is at room temperature. Cold-process soaps need to be stamped right after being cut into individual bars.

How do I emboss bars of soap?

Embossing your soap with a rubber stamp creates a wonderful added accent to your finished bars. The stamp can be re-attached to the mount and used to stamp matching packaging for gift giving.

Embossed Soap Bars
by Marie Browning

Here's How:

1. Prepare the rubber stamp by carefully peeling it from the wooden base.

2. Using rubber cement, glue the rubber stamp, right side up, into the bottom of the mold.

3. Refer back to Technique 1: Steps 1–7 on pages 25–26.

4. Refer back to Technique 2: Step 2 on page 29, adding the liquid colorant of your choice to the melted soap base.

5. Refer back to Technique 1: Step 8 on page 26, adding the scented oil of your choice to the melted soap base.

6. Refer back to Technique 1: Steps 9–10 on page 27.

   Note: The rubber stamp usually comes out of the mold with the soap.

7. Using a corsage pin, carefully pry the rubber stamp from the bar of soap.

Design Tip: When choosing a rubber stamp, choose a deeply cut stamp with a clean edge.

7
technique

What You Need To Get Started:

Cooking oil spray
Corsage pin
Disposable chopstick, bamboo
Glycerin melt-and-pour soap base:
  Any color
Heat-resistant glass measuring cup
Kitchen knife, sharp unserrated
Liquid colorant:
  Any color
Molds
Rubber cement
Rubber stamp
Scented oil:
  Any fragrance
Skillet, deep

8
technique

**What You Need
To Get Started:**

Cooking oil spray
Disposable chopstick,
 bamboo
Glycerin melt-and-pour
soap bases:
 Blue transparent
 Green transparent
 Purple transparent
 Red transparent
 Yellow transparent,
 2 oz. each
 White opaque, 1$\frac{1}{2}$ lb.
Heat-resistant glass
 measuring cup
Kitchen knife,
 sharp unserrated
Mold:
 Half-round loaf,
 7$\frac{1}{2}$" long x
 4$\frac{1}{4}$" wide x 2" deep
Scented oils:
 Raspberry fragrance,
 $\frac{1}{4}$ tsp.
 Vanilla fragrance,
 $\frac{3}{8}$ tsp.
Skillet, deep

How do I add chunks of glycerin melt-and-pour soap base into melted soap base to create one-of-a-kind bars of soap?

Adding multicolored bits and pieces of transparent
soap base into a melted opaque soap base produces colorful bars of soap. When sliced, each bar of soap is different
because of the sizes and colors of soap chunks that
were used.

Kaleidoscope
Melt-and-Pour Soap Bars

Here's How:

1. Using a sharp kitchen knife, cut all colors of transparent soap base into ½" and 1" irregular-shaped pieces. Set aside.

2. Refer back to Technique 1: Steps 1–8 on pages 25–26, using the white opaque soap base and both scented oils.

3. Pour a ¼" layer of the melted soap base into prepared mold.

Step 5

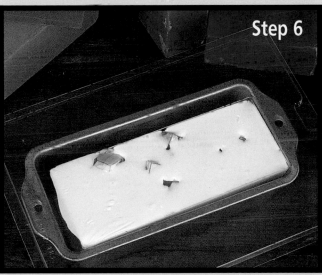

Step 6

Step 4

4. Randomly place the colored transparent pieces into the mold.

   Note: These soap base pieces should fill the mold ⅓" below the edge.

5. Refer back to Technique 1: Steps 9–10 on page 27, pouring the remaining melted soap base into prepared mold, covering all colored transparent pieces.

6. Using the sharp kitchen knife, slice the soap into individual bars.

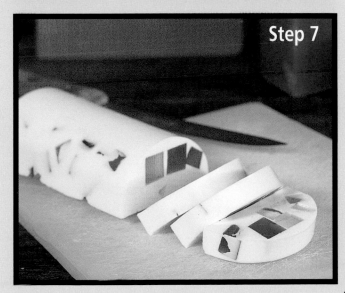

Step 7

9
technique

What You Need
To Get Started:

Cooking oil spray
Disposable chopstick,
    bamboo
Glycerin melt-and-pour
soap bases:
    Clear transparent, 3/4 lb.
    Green opaque, scraps
    White opaque, 1/4 lb.
2 Heat-resistant glass
    measuring cups
Iridescent powder:
    Clear
Kitchen knife,
    sharp unserrated
Liquid colorants:
    Blue
    Red
Molds:
    4 Ovals, 3 oz.
    Tiny hearts
Potato peeler
Rubbing alcohol
Scented oils:
    Papaya fragrance,
        1/8 tsp.
    Plum fragrance,
        1/8 tsp.
Skillet, deep
Spray bottle
Toothpick

How do I mold glycerin melt-and-pour soap base into tiny bars of soap and then embed them into larger bars of soap?

Tiny bars of soap can be individually molded or cut out with cookie cutters, then placed "inside" larger bars of soap. Opaque shapes can be placed inside transparent bars and vice versa. In addition, soap shavings can also be placed as a decorative element inside bars of soap.

Tiny Heart and Iridescent Transparent Melt-and-Pour Soap Bars

Here's How:

1. Refer back to Technique 1: Steps 1–7 on pages 25–26, using the tiny hearts mold and the white opaque soap base.

2. Refer back to Technique 2: Step 2 on page 29, adding twelve drops blue and four drops red liquid colorant to the melted soap base.

3. Refer back to Technique 1: Steps 9–10 on page 27.

4. Using a potato peeler, shave the green opaque soap base until you have an ample amount of shavings.

5. Refer back to Technique 1: Steps 1–8, using the oval molds, the clear transparent soap base, and the scented oils.

6. Place a pinch of iridescent powder into the melted soap base. Using the chopstick, gently stir to evenly distribute the powder.

7. Pour a 1/4" layer of the melted soap base into prepared molds.

8. Place the tiny heart bars of soap, molded side down, and the green soap shavings into the mold. Using a toothpick, push the hearts and the shavings down into the layer of melted soap base and adjust as desired.

Step 8

9. Spray a light mist of rubbing alcohol on top of the transparent layer, tiny heart bars of soap, and green soap shavings.

Note: Make certain to coat the layer of soap evenly to assure the soap layers bond together and do not separate.

10. Refer back to Technique 1: Steps 9–10, pouring the remaining melted soap base into prepared molds, covering all tiny heart bars of soap and green soap shavings.

How do I embed decorative objects into glycerin melt-and-pour bars of soap?

A decorative effect is achieved when objects are embedded into bars of soap. There are many objects that work well for this purpose. Choose jewelry or seashells, or delight a child by using a small plastic toy. The finished bar of soap will look much like a clear paperweight.

Sea-life Melt-and-Pour Soap Bars

Here's How:

1. Using a potato peeler, shave the green transparent and green opaque soap base until you have an ample amount of shavings. Shape the shavings to resemble sea grass.

2. Refer back to Technique 1: Steps 1–8 on pages 25–26, using the clear transparent soap base and the scented oils.

3. Pour a 1/4" layer of the melted soap base into prepared molds.

4. Place the plastic sea-life figures and the green soap shavings into the mold. Using a toothpick, push the plastic figures and the shavings down into the layer of melted soap base and adjust as desired.

5. Using a paring knife, cut one thin piece of green opaque soap base to go along the bottoms of the oval- and rectangular-shaped molds to resemble the bottom of the ocean. Position these pieces in place.

6. Refer back to Technique 1: Steps 1–7, using the blue transparent soap base.

7. Spray a light mist of rubbing alcohol on top of the clear transparent layer, plastic figures, green soap shavings, and thin pieces of soap base.

   Note: Make certain to coat the layer of soap evenly to assure the soap layers bond together and do not separate.

8. Refer back to Technique 1: Steps 9–10 on page 27, pouring the blue transparent melted soap base into prepared molds, covering all plastic figures and green soap shavings.

**What You Need
To Get Started:**

Cooking oil spray
Disposable chopstick, bamboo
Glycerin melt-and-pour soap bases:
  Blue transparent, 1/2 lb.
  Clear transparent, 1/2 lb.
  Green opaque, scraps
  Green transparent, scraps
2 Heat-resistant glass measuring cups
Kitchen knife, sharp unserrated
Molds:
  Circle
  Oval
  Rectangle
Paring knife
3 Plastic sea-life figures
Potato peeler
Rubbing alcohol
Scented oils:
  Eucalyptus fragrance, 1/8 tsp.
  Lavender essential, 1/8 tsp.
Skillet, deep
Spray bottle
Toothpick

How do I fully or partially embed oversized decorative objects into glycerin melt-and-pour bars of soap?

Plastic bath toys can be fully or partially embedded in soap using a common plastic storage container as the mold. A rubber duck can be completely immersed in the soap and emerge as the soap is used. A rubber dolphin—partially embedded—appears to be coming up out of the ocean.

Rubber Duck and Dolphin Melt-and-Pour Soap Bars

Here's How:

1. Refer back to Technique 1: Steps 1–8 on pages 25–26, using the round container mold, the clear transparent soap base, and the rain fragrance scented oil.

2. Pour a ³/₄" layer of the melted soap base into prepared mold.

3. Place the rubber duck into the mold. Gently push it down into the layer of melted soap base and adjust as desired.

4. Spray a light mist of rubbing alcohol on top of the clear transparent layer and rubber duck.

   Note: Make certain to coat the layer of soap evenly to assure the soap layers bond together and do not separate.

5. Refer back to Technique 1: Steps 9–10 on page 27, pouring the remaining clear transparent melted soap base into prepared mold, completely covering the rubber duck.

6. Refer back to Technique 1: Steps 1–8, using the square container mold, the blue transparent soap base, and the ocean fragrance scented oil.

7. Pour a 1¹/₂"-2" layer of the melted soap base into prepared mold.

8. Place the rubber dolphin into the mold. Gently push it down into the layer of melted soap base and adjust as desired.

9. Refer back to Technique 1: Step 10.

> *Design Tip: The depth of the mold will depend on the size of the object being fully or partially embedded.*

What You Need To Get Started:

Cooking oil spray
Disposable chopstick, bamboo
Glycerin melt-and-pour soap bases:
  Blue transparent, ³/₄ lb.
  Clear transparent, 1 lb.
2 Heat-resistant glass measuring cups
Kitchen knife, sharp unserrated
Molds:
  Plastic container, 3" diameter x 4" deep
  Plastic container, 4" square x 3" deep
Rubber dolphin
Rubber duck
Rubbing alcohol
Scented oils:
  Ocean fragrance, ¹/₄ tsp.
  Rain fragrance, ³/₈ tsp.
Skillet, deep
Spray bottle

12
technique

Cooking oil spray
Disposable chopstick,
  bamboo
Glycerin melt-and-pour
soap bases:
  Clear transparent, ¼ lb.
  Purple opaque, ½ lb.
  Purple transparent, 1 lb.
Heat-resistant glass
  measuring cup
Kitchen knife,
  sharp unserrated
Masking tape
Molds:
  Plastic container,
    8" long x
    4" wide x ?" deep
  PVC® pipe,
    3" diameter x 8" long
Plastic wrap
Preformed soap shape,
  white "S"
Rubber bands
Rubbing alcohol
Scented oil:
  Plum fragrance, ½ tsp.
Skillet, deep
Spray bottle

How do I embed
a preformed soap shape into
a glycerin melt-and-pour
loaf of soap?

Embedding a continuous preformed soap shape into a loaf of soap allows several bars of soap with a similar design to be molded at one time. The basic designs in this soap will vary throughout the loaf, adding interest.

Preformed Shape Melt-and-Pour Soap Bars

Here's How:

1. Refer back to Technique 1: Steps 1–7 on pages 25–26, using the rectangular container mold and the purple opaque soap base.

2. Refer back to Technique 1: Steps 9–10 on page 27.

3. Using the sharp kitchen knife, slice the soap into three strips. One strip should measure 8" long, 1½" wide, and ⅛" deep. The remaining two strips should measure 8" long, ¼" wide, and ¼" deep.

4. Cut the preformed soap shape in half lengthwise.

   Note: Cutting the soap shape evenly is not important. Any variation in the basic design will add interest to the soap after it has been sliced into individual bars.

5. Prepare the pipe by spraying the inside with cooking oil. Wipe away excess oil.

6. Tear three pieces of plastic wrap large enough to cover one end of the pipe plus approximately 2" to secure it around the sides.

7. Place the pieces of plastic wrap over one end of the pipe and tightly stretch. Hold in place with rubber bands, then secure with masking tape to make certain the plastic wrap is thoroughly attached to the pipe.

8. Place the wrapped end of the pipe on a flat surface so it is standing up.

9. Refer back to Technique 1: Steps 2–8, using the clear and purple transparent soap bases.

10. Pour a 1" layer of the melted soap base into prepared pipe mold.

11. Place the three purple opaque soap strips and the preformed soap shape halves into the mold. Hold in place until the soap shapes stand on their own.

    Note: Make certain to leave enough space between the soap shapes so the melted

Step 11

soap base can fill in around the shapes to prevent the soap shapes from falling out when the soap is sliced into individual bars.

12. Spray a light mist of rubbing alcohol into the pipe to cover all soap shapes and the transparent layer.

    Note: Make certain to coat the layer of soap evenly to assure the soap layers bond together and do not separate.

13. Refer back to Technique 1: Step 9, pouring the remaining melted soap base into the pipe, covering all of the soap shapes.

14. Remove the plastic wrap from the end of the pipe and gently press the soap out of the mold.

    Note: If the soap does not easily release, a butter knife, gently run around the sealed edges, may help loosen it.

15. Using the sharp kitchen knife, slice the soap into individual bars.

Design Tip: When using PVC® pipe as a soap mold, keep in mind that it will take longer for the soap to cool and solidify than when using a plastic mold.

Coté
Bastide
Bain
de bleuets
des
champs,
500 ml
Made in France

How do I use the rebatching method to make bars of soap?

Soap can be made by using grated cold-process soap that has been mixed with liquid (in this case, goat's milk) and slow-heated until they are combined. Grated cold-process soap which gives the same benefits and aesthetics as homemade cold-process soap can also be purchased.

The advantages to making rebatched soap is that you can make one large batch and divide it up into several smaller batches of soap featuring different colors and/or scents.

Honey/Oatmeal Rebatched Soap Bars

Here's How:

1. Prepare mold by spraying the inside with cooking oil. Wipe away excess oil.

2. Place grated soap and milk in a crockpot and heat on low for 45 minutes.

3. Using a wooden spoon, stir the grated soap and milk mixture.

    Note: If the milk has been fully absorbed and the mixture is the consistency of oatmeal, it is ready to be molded. If it is not ready, continue to heat, checking at 15-minute intervals. If the mixture appears too dry, a small amount of liquid may be added.

    If the mixture is heated at too high a temperature or for too long, it may turn orange. To help prevent this, make certain the contents in the crockpot fill it at least half way. The "orange color" will only affect the visual appearance of the soap.

    If the mixture is too lumpy, a wire whisk can be used at this point to work out the lumps.

What You Need To Get Started:

Botanical:
  Oatmeal,
  1/2 cup finely ground
Cold-process soap:
  Unscented,
  2 lb. grated
Cooking oil spray
Cooling rack
Crockpot, 2 qt.
Cutting board
Goat's milk, 16 oz.
Honey, 2 tbsp.
Kitchen knife,
  sharp unserrated
Mold:
  Plastic container,
  9" long x
  5" wide x 3 1/2" deep
Plastic spatula
Scented oils:
  Chamomile fragrance,
  1/2 tsp.
  Vanilla fragrance,
  1 tsp.
Wooden spoon

4. Add scented oils and honey to the melted mixture. Using the wooden spoon, gently stir to evenly distribute the fragrance and the honey.

5. Add oatmeal to the melted mixture. Using the wooden spoon, stir until the oatmeal is well mixed into the mixture.

6. Pour the melted soap mixture into prepared mold. Using a plastic spatula, gently press the mixture into the mold.

   Caution: Make certain to press thoroughly to avoid air pockets from forming in the mixture.

7. Allow the soap to cool, uncovered, until solidified (approximately 24–48 hours).

8. Turn the mold over and release the soap.

9. Place the soap onto a large cutting board that has been dedicated to soapmaking. Using a sharp kitchen knife, slice the soap into individual bars.

10. Place the bars of soap on a cooling rack and allow to cure for three to four weeks.

How do I use the rebatching method to make balls of soap with botanical infusions?

Using the rebatching method is one of the easiest ways to make soap balls. The rebatched soap can be divided, allowing for each division to feature a different color or scent.

In this case, the liquid being added to the grated cold-process soap is an infusion that has been derived from a botanical which has been allowed to steep. This is a good way to get the benefits of an herb, such as antiseptic and astringent, without having the "bulk" in the soap.

Rosemary/Orange/Chamomile Infused Soap Balls

Here's How:

1. Bring the distilled water to a boil in a saucepan.

2. Place the rosemary botanical into a glass jar.

3. Using a measuring cup with a pouring spout, pour the boiling distilled water into the glass jar.

4. Place the lid on the glass jar and allow the rosemary infusion to steep (a minimum of 4 hours). Strain the steeped rosemary infusion to remove the bulk.

Note: Making the rosemary infusion the night before it is to be used is recommended to assure it has been allowed to steep properly.

5. Preheat oven to 180°F. Place grated soap and $3/4$ cup rosemary infusion in a covered casserole dish and heat in oven for 45 minutes.

6. Using a wooden spoon, stir the grated soap and rosemary infusion mixture.

What You Need To Get Started:

Botanicals:
  Chamomile, 1 tbsp.
  Rosemary, $1^1/_2$ tbsp.
Cold-process soap:
  Unscented,
  1 lb. grated
Cookie sheet
Cooking oil spray
Cooling rack
Covered casserole dish
Distilled water, 1 cup
Glass canning jar
  with lid, 1 pint
Liquid colorant:
  Orange
Measuring cup
  with pouring spout
Saucepan
Scented oil:
  Orange essential,
  $1^1/_2$ tsp.
Strainer
Waxed paper
Wooden spoon

Note: If the rosemary infusion has been fully absorbed and the mixture is the consistency of oatmeal, it is ready to be molded. If it is not ready, continue to heat, checking at 5-minute intervals. If the mixture appears too dry, a small amount of liquid may be added.

If the mixture is heated at too high a temperature or for too long, it may turn orange. To help prevent this, make certain the contents in the casserole dish fill it at least half way. The "orange color" will only affect the visual appearance of the soap.

7. Refer back to Technique 2: Step 2 on page 29, adding nine drops (or more, if desired) orange liquid colorant to the melted soap base. Mix with the wooden spoon.

8. Refer back to Technique 1: Step 8 on page 26. Mix with the wooden spoon.

9. Using the wooden spoon, thoroughly stir in the chamomile.

10. Allow to cool until the soap can be handled and will hold its shape.

11. Prepare cookie sheet by covering with waxed paper.

12. Spray your hands with cooking oil and mold the soap into balls. The balls can be any size desired. Place individual balls onto cookie sheet.

13. Over the next 24 hours, periodically rotate the balls to prevent them from getting a flat side. Remold by hand as necessary.

14. Place the balls of soap on a cooling rack and allow to cure for three to four weeks.

To make the rosemary/lemon infused balls of soap, refer back to the "Here's How" instructions on pages 53–54, substituting four drops of yellow liquid colorant for the orange liquid colorant. In addition, substitute 1 tsp. lemon essential and ¹/₄ tsp. rosemary essential scented oils for the orange essential scented oil and the chamomile botanical.

How do I use the cold-process method to make basic soap?

When making basic soap, using the cold-process method, it is a chemical reaction between the lye and the melted fats that makes this possible. Just about any fat or combination of fats may be used when making cold-process soap. Soap qualities—such as the hardness or softness of the bar, whether it is harsh or mild, the size and amount of bubbles it produces—are determined by the types of fats used. The amount of lye used is determined by the saponification value of each fat and the quantity of the fats to be used.

Saponification charts are available in more advanced soapmaking manuals when you become more adventurous and wish to do some experimenting in creating your own soap formulas.

What You Need To Get Started:

Bath towels
Blanket
Cooling rack
Cutting board
Disposable chopstick, bamboo
Distilled water
Fats:
  Coconut oil
  Olive oil
  Vegetable shortening
Glass juice jar with lid, 48 oz.
Hammer
Kitchen knife, sharp unserrated
Laboratory thermometer (with stainless steel shaft), 0° to 180° F
Large nail
Latex gloves
Lye crystals
Masking tape
Measuring cup with pouring spout
Mold:
  Plastic or wooden container with lid
Plastic garbage bag
Protective eyewear
Scale (must be able to weigh up to 5 lb.)
Scented oils:
  Eucalyptus fragrance, 1 tsp.
  Peppermint fragrance, 2 tsp.
Stainless steel stockpot, 12 qt.
Wooden spoon

One Batch of Basic Cold-process Soap Recipe

Distilled water, 33 oz.
Fats:
  Coconut oil, 22 oz.
  Olive oil, 29 oz.
  Shortening, 38 oz.
Lye crystals, 12 oz.
Mold: 11" long x 9" wide x 3" deep

Note: When using lye, use only glass, plastic, stainless steel, or wood—aluminum must not be used. In addition, do not substitute liquid lye for lye crystals.

Eucalyptus/Peppermint Cold-process Soap Bars

Here's How:

1. Prepare mold by lining with a plastic garbage bag. Using masking tape, secure the garbage bag in place.

   Caution: Make certain the garbage bag is as free of wrinkles as possible to prevent creases from forming in the soap.

2. Using a hammer and a large nail, punch two holes in the lid of the glass jar, large enough for the thermometer shaft to pass through.

   Note: When the lid is placed on the jar, these holes will allow the contents to breathe.

3. Place the glass jar in the kitchen sink. Using a measuring cup with a pouring spout, measure and pour 33 oz. of distilled water into the glass jar.

4. Thoroughly dry the measuring cup and place it on the scale. Adjust the scale to zero so it does not weigh the measuring cup. Carefully pour the lye crystals into the measuring cup until it weighs 12 oz.

   Caution: Lye (sodium hydroxide) is a caustic soda and can be fatal if swallowed. Keep lye out of the reach of children. When working with lye, make certain to wear latex gloves and protective eyewear. Be careful not to breathe in any lye crystals as they can cause serious burns to sensitive tissues.

5. Carefully pour the lye crystals into the glass jar of water.

   Caution: Water should never be poured into lye. It should always be the lye that is added to the water. If the skin comes into contact with lye, it will begin to feel slippery, itch, and/or burn. If any of these sensations occur, immediately rinse the area with vinegar and then running water. If the lye splashes into your eyes, immediately follow the manufacturer's directions on the lye container. Lye can also remove paint. If any should splatter onto a painted work surface, wash it off imme-diately with water and a mild detergent.

6. Using a disposable chopstick, gently stir the water and lye solution until the lye crystals are completely dissolved.

   Caution: If the lye crystals do not dissolve completely, hazardous chunks of lye can be left in the finished soap.

7. Place the lid (with holes) on the glass jar. The lye solution will immediately begin to heat up and the glass jar will become very hot. It will take the solution several hours to cool—making the solution in the evening and allowing it to cool overnight works well.

   Caution: Do not attempt to move the glass jar from the kitchen sink while the jar is hot. Keep out of the reach of children and pets! It is also a good idea to label the jar with a warning so that family members are not in any danger.

8. Once the lye solution has cooled down, place the shaft of the thermometer into one of the holes in the lid and measure the temperature of the solution. You want the solution to be 105°F. If the solution needs to be warmed up, a warm water bath may be necessary. If the solution needs to be cooled down, a cool water bath may be necessary.

   Note: The thermometer that you are using must be extremely accurate as the temperatures of the lye solution and of the melted fats are critical.

9. At the same time you are getting the lye solution to 105°F, the fats need to be prepared. Refer back to recipe on page 55. Place all of the fats into a stainless steel stockpot and heat on low until the fats are barely melted. Measure the temperature of the fats. You want the fats to be 105°F.

   Caution: The temperatures of the fats and the lye solution must be exactly the same.

It may be easier to use two separate thermometers—one for the melted fats, the other for the lye solution.

10. When the fully melted fats and the lye solution reach the same temperatures, they are ready to be combined.

    Caution: Turn the burners on the stove off.

11. Remove the stockpot from the stove and slowly pour the lye solution into the fats, stirring constantly with a wooden spoon. When the lye solution and the fats are combined, there will be a noticeable change in the consistency of the mixture.

    Caution: Make certain to wear latex gloves and protective eyewear.

Step 12

Step 11

13. Add scented oils to the mixture. Using the wooden spoon, gently stir to evenly distribute the fragrance.

14. Immediately pour the mixture into prepared mold and place the lid on the mold. Do not cover the top of the mixture with the plastic garbage bag—leave the plastic hanging over the edges of the mold.

    Caution: If there is too much time taken between trace and pouring the mixture into the mold, the soap could begin to set up in the stockpot.

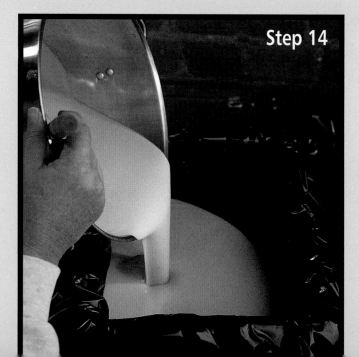
Step 14

12. Continue stirring until the mixture begins to "trace." This process can take from 20 to 90 minutes.

    Note: Trace means when the mixture becomes thick enough that when drizzled from the wooden spoon onto the surface of the remaining mixture in the stockpot, it will leave a visible trail before it disappears.

15. Cover the mold with bath towels and a blanket to keep the soap at a controlled temperature. Place it out of any drafty areas and allow to cool until solidified (a minimum of 24 hours).

    Caution: If the soap is allowed to cool too quickly it will not set-up properly. Do not get impatient, the soap must be allowed to sit undisturbed for a minimum of 24 hours.

16. After the initial 24 hours, unwrap the mold and remove the lid. Test the soap with your fingers to see if it is firm. If the soap is not set-up, replace the lid and rewrap the mold with the bath towels. Allow to sit for an additional 24 hours.

17. Lift the plastic garbage bag and the soap out of the mold.

Step 17

18. Place the soap onto a large cutting board that has been dedicated to soapmaking. Using a sharp kitchen knife, slice the soap into individual bars.

19. Place the bars of soap on a cooling rack and allow to cure for three to four weeks.

    Note: A thin, powdery surface on top of the soap is common and can be trimmed off. However, if hard, shiny spots appear in the soap, it has not properly saponified and lye has been left in the soap. In this case, the soap must not be used! It is important to know that though lye is used to make soap, its caustic characteristics are altered during the saponification and curing processes.

Step 18

Step 19

Note: If you are making this soap for rebatching purposes, leave out the scented oils and grate after unmolding.

How do I make bubbling bath oil?

Handmade soap need not be limited to solid forms. Liquid soap bases can be purchased and personalized with favorite scents, as well as Vitamin E, glycerin, and almond or apricot oils for the benefits that they provide the skin.

The liquid soap and scented oils will separate to create an attractive layered look. Shake the bottle well before pouring the bubbling bath oil into your bath.

Tangerine Bubbling Bath Oil
by Marie Browning

Here's How:

1. Combine the liquid soap base, tangerine scented oil, and four drops red liquid colorant in a measuring cup with a pouring spout. Using a disposable chopstick, gently stir to thoroughly mix.

2. Add the glycerin, almond oil, and ten drops orange liquid colorant to the liquid soap mixture. Using the chopstick, gently stir to thoroughly mix.

3. Carefully pour the liquid soap mixture into the plastic bottle.

   Note: The liquid soap and scented oils will separate into two colored layers after approximately 30 minutes.

**What You Need
To Get Started:**

Almond oil, $\frac{1}{2}$ cup
Disposable chopstick, bamboo
Glycerin, 1 tbsp.
Liquid colorants:
  Orange
  Red
Liquid soap base, $\frac{1}{2}$ cup
Measuring cup with pouring spout
Plastic bottle with flip-top cap, 8 oz.
Scented oil:
  Tangerine fragrance, 20 drops

How do I make small bars of soap and frost them to resemble petit fours?

17
technique

Frosting soap is fun and easy! The results are simply beautiful and surprisingly real. These small bars of soap make wonderful bath and kitchen soap displays when placed in a small antique-type dish or bowl.

What You Need To Get Started:

Butter knife
Cake decorating book
Cooking oil spray
Cool water
Decorating tips
Disposable chopstick, bamboo
Electric mixer
Eye droppers
Frosting bag
Frosting soap bar
Glycerin melt-and-pour soap base:
  White opaque
Heat-resistant glass measuring cup
Kitchen knife, sharp unserrated
Liquid colorants:
  Blue
  Green
  Red
  Yellow
Measuring spoons
Mold:
  Petit four
Mixing bowl, large
Plastic spatula
Scented oils:
  Fruit-flavored scents
Skillet, deep
Waxed paper

Frosted Petit Four Soap
by Soapsations / Yaley Enterprises

Here's How:

1. Refer back to Technique 1: Steps 1–7 on pages 25–26, using the white opaque soap base.

2. Refer back to Technique 2: Step 2 on page 29, adding just enough liquid colorant to the melted soap base to render the desired shade of pastel.

   Note: You will want to make blue, green, pink, and yellow bars of soap.

3. Refer back to Technique 1: Step 8 on page 26, adding just enough scented oil to the melted soap base to render the desired fragrance.

4. Refer back to Technique 1: Steps 9–10 on page 27. Place the soap bars on a sheet of waxed paper and set aside.

5. Refer back to Technique 1: Steps 2–7, using half of the frosting soap bar.

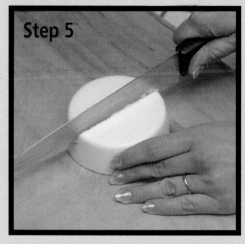

Step 5

Note: The melted soap mixture should have a milky appearance.

6. Pour the melted frosting soap into a large mixing bowl.

   Note: One-quarter cup will more than triple in size when it is whipped.

7. Quickly add 2½ tablespoons of cool water to the melted frosting soap before the soap begins to set-up.

Note: This will help prevent lumps from forming which will clog the decorating tip.

8. Using an electric mixer, immediately begin whipping the frosting soap on low speed. The soap will become bubbly, then creamy, then start to rise. Continue whipping on medium speed until the soap becomes a fluffy, dry texture similar to icing.

   Note: The more you whip the soap, the fluffier it becomes and the easier it is to use. Whipping time is approximately three to four minutes before the frosting soap is ready to use.

Step 8

Notes:

   If you find that the frosting is too dry and is hard to push out of the frosting bag, just add five to ten more drops of cool water to the whipped frosting and mix well. This will soften the frosting.

   The whipped soap can be stored for several months in an air-tight zipper lock bag in the refrigerator.

9. Using an eye dropper, add liquid colorant to the whipped frosting. Using a butter knife, gently stir to evenly distribute the color.

   Note: When using two or more colors to render the desired color, use a separate eye dropper for each color of liquid colorant.

Step 9

10. Place the scallop tip on the frosting bag. Using a plastic spatula, fill the frosting bag with the colored frosting.

11. Trim around the edge of several petit four soaps.

12. Using the appropriate tips and colors of frosting, embellish the top of each soap with a flower and a couple leaves.

    Note: The instructions for a number of various flowers and leaves can be found in any cake decorating book.

Caution: If children will be using the soap, use a perfume-type fragrance and not a fruit-flavored scent. The soap just might be too tempting to resist!

Section 3:
projects

How do I mold soap-on-a-rope?

1 project

Using the rebatching method, this novel approach is the basis for making his and hers soaps on a rope. Each one is customized with scented oils and botanicals to complement the characteristics of each gender.

What You Need To Get Started:

Cold-process soap:
 Unscented,
 1 lb. grated
Cookie sheet
Cooking oil spray
Cooling rack
Covered casserole dish
Glass mixing bowl
Measuring cup
Milk, ³/₄ cup
Waxed paper
Wooden spoon

His and Hers Soaps-on-a-Rope

Here's How:

1. Preheat oven to 180°F. Place grated soap and milk in a covered casserole dish and heat in oven for 45 minutes.

2. Refer back to Technique 13: Step 3 on page 51.

3. Divide the soap mixture in half, placing half the mixture into a glass mixing bowl.

4. **To make his soap:** Add five drops green liquid colorant to the melted soap mixture in the casserole dish. Using the wooden spoon, gently stir to evenly distribute the color.

5. Add bay rum fragrance and lime essential scented oils to the melted mixture. Using the wooden spoon, gently stir to evenly distribute the fragrances.

6. Thoroughly stir in the grated lime peel. Set aside to cool.

7. **To make her soap:** Add two drops red liquid colorant to the melted soap mixture in the glass mixing bowl. Using the wooden spoon, gently stir to evenly distribute the color.

8. Add rosebud fragrance and sandalwood essential scented oils to the melted mixture. Using the wooden spoon, gently stir to evenly distribute the fragrances.

9. Thoroughly stir in the dried rose petals. Set aside to cool.

His Soap:
Botanical:
 Fresh lime peel,
 grated
Cotton cording,
 ¹/₃ yd.
Liquid colorant:
 Green
Scented oils:
 Bay rum fragrance,
 ¹/₂ tsp.
 Lime essential,
 ¹/₄ tsp.

Her Soap:
Botanicals:
 3 Rose buds, dried
 Rose petals,
 1¹/₂ tbsp. dried
Liquid colorant:
 Red
Ribbon, 1 yd.
Scented oils:
 Rosebud fragrance,
 ¹/₂ tsp.
 Sandalwood essential,
 ¹/₈ tsp.

10. Refer back to Technique 14: Steps 10–12 on page 54. The hanging device must be added while you are molding the soap into balls.

11. **For his soap:** Fold a length of cotton cording in half and tie a knot at the ends. When molding the soap, make certain to leave the entire knot showing, allowing the cording to run through the center of the soap, extending out the top of the ball.

12. **For her soap:** Fold a 7" length of ribbon in half and tie a knot at the ends. When molding the soap, leave only the "loop" extending out the top of the ball.

13. Press the dried rose buds into the soap for a decorative effect. Thread the remaining length of ribbon through the loop and tie a knot at the ends.

14. Refer back to Technique 14: Steps 13–14 on page 54.

How do I mold glycerin melt-and-pour soap base inside a loofah sponge?

Soap molded inside a loofah sponge combines the benefits of using a natural sponge and a gentle soap made with kelp to add soothing and healing qualities for healthier skin.

2 project

What You Need To Get Started:

Botanical:
  Powdered kelp, 1½ tsp.
Disposable chopstick,
  bamboo
Duct tape
Glycerin melt-and-pour
soap base:
  White opaque, 1 lb.
Heat-resistant glass
  measuring cup
Kitchen knife,
  sharp serrated
Kitchen knife,
  sharp unserrated
Loofah sponge
Plastic wrap
Rubber bands
Scented oil:
  Rain fragrance, ¾ tsp.
Skillet, deep

Rain-scented Soap Inside a Loofah Sponge

Here's How:

1. Using a sharp serrated kitchen knife, slice the loofah sponge into three 1½" slices.

2. Tear two pieces of plastic wrap large enough to cover one end of each loofah sponge slice plus approximately 1½" to secure it around the sides.

3. Place the pieces of plastic wrap over one end of each loofah sponge slice and tightly stretch. Hold in place with rubber bands, then secure with duct tape to make certain the plastic wrap is thoroughly attached to the loofah.

4. Refer back to Technique 1: Steps 2–8 on pages 25–26.

5. Add the powdered kelp to the melted soap base. Using the chopstick, gently stir to evenly distribute the color.

6. Pour the melted soap base into the holes in the loofah sponge slices and allow to cool until solidified.

7. Remove the plastic wrap from the ends of the loofah sponge slices.

8. If necessary, scrape excess soap from the sides of the loofah sponge slices.

Design Tip: Peppermint, eucalyptus, and rosemary essential oils are pleasant as alternative fragrances. They can be used alone or in any combination.

How do I accent the raised design of a mold with a different color than the actual bar of soap?

When using a mold with a raised design, it is oftentimes important to mold the details of the design in a different color to help them stand out. In this case, the molds have Japanese kanji. Rice flour and green tea are added for an authentic oriental touch.

Japanese Tea Soap Bars

Here's How:

1. Refer back to Technique 1: Steps 1–7 on pages 25–26, using only 2 oz. of the white opaque soap base.

2. Refer back to Technique 2: Step 2 on page 29, adding one drop blue and six drops orange liquid colorant to the melted soap base.

3. Pour the melted soap base into prepared molds, filling only the areas of the raised designs, and allow to cool until solidified.

4. Using the edge of a flat plastic card, carefully scrape and remove the excess soap from the mold.

   Note: A credit card works great for this purpose.

5. Refer back to Technique 1: Steps 1–8, using the remaining white opaque soap base.

6. Add the rice flour and the contents from the tea bag to the melted soap base. Using the chopstick, gently stir to evenly distribute.

7. Spray a light mist of rubbing alcohol on top of the soap in the molds.

   Note: Make certain to coat the layer of soap evenly to assure the soap layers bond together and do not separate.

8. Refer back to Technique 1: Step 9 on page 27.

   Note: The majority of the green tea leaves will sink to the bottom of the mold.

9. Refer back to Technique 1: Step 10 on page 27.

What You Need To Get Started:

Cooking oil spray
Disposable chopstick, bamboo
Glycerin melt-and-pour soap base:
  White opaque, 1 lb.
Green tea bag
2 Heat-resistant glass measuring cups
Kitchen knife, sharp unserrated
Liquid colorants:
  Blue
  Orange
Molds:
  3 Japanese with raised designs, 4 oz.
Plastic card, flat
Rice flour, 2 tbsp.
Rubbing alcohol
Scented oil:
  Green tea fragrance, $1/4$ tsp.
Skillet, deep
Spray bottle

73

How do I embed preformed soap shapes into a layered glycerin melt-and-pour loaf of soap?

Embedding a preformed soap shape into a loaf of soap that has been layered with different colors of melt-and-pour soap base makes for a visually appealing loaf. In fact, as a decorative element, slice only a couple bars from the loaf and display the remaining.

Pear-scented Soap Loaf and Bars

Here's How:

1. Refer back to Technique 1: Steps 1–7 on pages 25–26, using the yellow transparent soap base.

2. Pour the melted soap base into prepared mold and allow to cool until solidified enough to handle—it should still be slightly warm.

3. Turn the mold over and release the soap. Gently mold the soap into a squiggly shape from the eight-inch side. Set aside and allow to finish cooling and setting up.

4. Using the sharp kitchen knife, cut the green transparent soap base into three 6" strips.

5. Using a grater, finely grate the yellow opaque soap base to make $1/2$ cup.

6. Refer back to Technique 1: Steps 1–7, using the clear transparent soap base.

7. Place a pinch of iridescent powder into the melted soap base. Using the chopstick, gently stir to evenly distribute the powder.

8. Quickly stir in the grated yellow soap base.

9. Pour the melted soap base into prepared mold.

10. Place the yellow transparent preformed soap shape and one of the green transparent soap strips into the mold. Hold in place until the preformed soap shape stands on its own. Allow to cool until solidified.

11. Refer back to Technique 1: Steps 1–7, using the white opaque soap base.

What You Need To Get Started:

Cooking oil spray
Disposable chopstick, bamboo
Glycerin melt-and-pour soap bases:
 Clear transparent, $3/4$ lb.
 Green transparent, scraps
 White opaque, $1 1/2$ lb.
 Yellow opaque, scraps
 Yellow transparent, $1/2$ lb.
Grater
Heat-resistant glass measuring cup
Iridescent powder:
 Clear
Kitchen knife, sharp unserrated
Liquid colorants:
 Green
 Yellow
Mold:
 Plastic container, 8" long x 6" wide x 6" deep
Rubbing alcohol
Scented oil:
 Pear fragrance, $3/4$ tsp.
Skillet, deep
Spray bottle

75

12. Refer back to Technique 2: Step 2 on page 29, adding four drops green and thirty drops yellow liquid colorant to the melted soap base.

13. Refer back to Technique 1: Step 8 on page 26.

14. Spray a light mist of rubbing alcohol on top of the clear layer with grated yellow soap and to cover all soap shapes.

    Note: Make certain to coat the layer of soap evenly to assure the soap layers bond together and do not separate.

15. Refer back to Technique 1: Step 9 on page 27, placing the remaining two green transparent soap strips as desired.

16. Refer back to Technique 1: Step 10 on page 27.

17. Using the sharp kitchen knife, slice the soap into individual bars. If desired, leave part of the loaf unsliced and display it near the cut bars.

project

What You Need To Get Started:

Cooking oil spray
Disposable chopstick, bamboo
Glycerin melt-and-pour soap base:
  White opaque, $^3/_4$ lb.
Gold powder
Heat-resistant glass measuring cup
Molds:
  5 Cherubs, 2 oz.
Paintbrush, small
Scented oil:
  Gardenia fragrance, $^3/_8$ tsp.
Skillet, deep

Gilded Cherub Soap

How do I accent the details of a mold with gold powder?

Highlighting detailed areas with gold powder is known as gilding. A small paintbrush—either flat or round—is used to brush the gold powder into the detailed areas, then the powder is allowed to settle into the crevices. In this case, the gilding adds an angelic touch to these heavenly cherub soaps.

Here's How:

1. Refer back to Technique 1: Step 1 on page 25.

2. Using a small, dry paintbrush, apply gold powder into the detailed areas of the molds and set aside.

3. Refer back to Technique 1: Steps 2–10 on pages 25–27.

How do I accent the raised design of a mold with gold leafing?

Soap can be gold-leafed to give it a rich, expensive look. The use of gold leafing adhesive is not necessary to apply the gold leafing because the surface of the soap is sticky enough to allow it to adhere properly. Frankincense and myrrh fragrances add even more richness and elegance to each bar of soap.

Gold-leafed Soap Bars

Here's How:

1. Refer back to Technique 1: Steps 1–7 on pages 25–26.

2. Refer back to Technique 2: Step 2 on page 29, adding three drops green and ten drops orange liquid colorant to the melted soap base.

3. Refer back to Technique 1: Step 8 on page 26.

4. Add the powdered myrrh to the melted soap base. Using the chopstick, gently stir to evenly distribute.

5. Refer back to Technique 1: Steps 9–10 on page 27.

6. Apply gold leafing on top of each bar of soap and gently rub with your finger to adhere. Remove excess gold leafing and set aside.

7. Continue rubbing the gold leafing until it is smooth and thoroughly bonded to the soap.

> *Design Tip: For a different effect, try using copper leafing.*

What You Need To Get Started:

Cooking oil spray
Disposable chopstick, bamboo
2 Gold leafing sheets
Glycerin melt-and-pour soap base:
    White opaque, 1 lb.
Heat-resistant glass measuring cup
Kitchen knife, sharp unserrated
Liquid colorants:
    Green
    Orange
Molds:
    4 Rectangular with raised designs, 5 oz.
Powdered myrrh, 1 tsp.
Scented oil:
    Frankincense/ myrrh fragrance, $3/8$ tsp.
Skillet, deep

7
project

What You Need To Get Started:

Cooking oil spray
Disposable chopstick,
  bamboo
Glycerin melt-and-pour
soap bases:
  Blue opaque, 1 lb.
  Blue transparent, $^1/_2$ lb.
  Red transparent, $^3/_4$ lb.
  White opaque, $^1/_4$ lb.
Heat-resistant glass
  measuring cup
Kitchen knife,
  sharp unserrated
Masking tape
Molds:
  Plastic container,
    6" long x
    4" wide x 4" deep
  PVC® pipe,
    $^3/_4$" diameter x 8" long
  PVC® pipe,
    $1^1/_4$" diameter x 8" long
Plastic wrap
Rubber bands
Rubbing alcohol
Scented oil:
  Ocean fragrance, $^3/_4$ tsp.
Skillet, deep
Spray bottle

How do I mold and create scenes in a glycerin melt-and-pour loaf of soap?

A full-length mold, like a PVC® pipe, needs to be used when creating a continuous scene in a loaf of soap. When the shape is removed from the pipe, it can be cut and placed into the soap to create designs or scenes. In this case, the circular shapes have been cut into halves (the sailboat) and quarters (the sails).

Sailboat Soap

Here's How:

1. Refer back to Technique 12: Steps 5–8 on page 49, preparing both pipe molds.

2. Refer back to Technique 1: Steps 2–7 on pages 25–26, using the 3/4"-diameter pipe mold and the white opaque soap base.

3. Refer back to Technique 1: Step 9 on page 27.

4. Refer back to Technique 12: Step 14 on page 49.

5. Refer back to Technique 1: Steps 2–7, using the 1 1/4"-diameter pipe mold and the red transparent soap base.

6. Refer back to Technique 1: Step 9.

7. Refer back to Technique 12: Step 14.

8. Using the sharp kitchen knife, cut the molded white soap into quarters lengthwise, creating four triangular shapes (for the sails). Cut the molded red soap in half lengthwise (for the sailboat). Cut one thin strip, lengthwise, from one of the halves (for the mast).

   Note: It may be necessary to trim the soap to a 6" length to fit into the rectangular container mold.

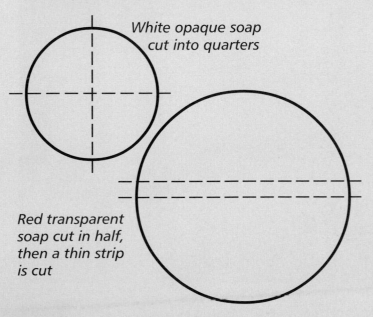

White opaque soap cut into quarters

Red transparent soap cut in half, then a thin strip is cut

9. Refer back to Technique 1: Steps 1–9, using the rectangular container mold, the blue transparent soap base, and 1/4 tsp. of the scented oil.

10. Before the layer of blue transparent soap has solidified, place the red semicircle in the middle, allowing it to float.

11. Refer back to Technique 1: Steps 2–8, using the blue opaque soap base and 1/2 tsp. of the scented oil.

12. Spray a light mist of rubbing alcohol on top of the transparent blue layer and the sailboat.

    Note: Make certain to coat the layer of soap evenly to assure the soap layers bond together and do not separate.

13. Pour half of the blue opaque soap base into the mold.

14. Place the thin red strip on the sailboat for the mast. Hold in place until the mast stands on its own.

15. Place one of the white quarter-circles against the mast for the lower sail. Hold in place until the sail stands on its own.

16. Spray a light mist of rubbing alcohol on top of the opaque blue layer, the sailboat, mast, and lower sail.

17. Pour the remaining half of the blue opaque soap base into the mold.

18. Place one of the white quarter-circles against the mast for the upper sail. Position this sail on the opposite side from the lower sail. Hold in place until the sail stands on its own.

19. Allow to cool until solidified.

20. Refer to Technique 1: Step 10 on page 27.

21. Using the sharp kitchen knife, slice the soap into individual bars.

How do I add botanicals to cold-process soap?

Botanicals added to cold-process soap add color, texture, and/or benefits to the skin. Calendula leaves have healing properties so are great for soaps made for sensitive skin.

Lavender/Mango/Tangerine Cold-process Soap Bars

Here's How:

1. Refer back to Technique 15: Steps 1–13 on pages 57–58, using the recipe at right, below.

2. Add ground calendula leaves to the traced mixture. Using the wooden spoon, stir until the leaves are well mixed into the mixture.

3. Refer back to Technique 15: Steps 14–19 on pages 58–59.

Design Tips:

Try using sunflower fragrance scented oil to complement the sunflower oil.

Try substituting ground chamomile for the calendula leaves.

What You Need To Get Started:

Bath towels
Blanket
Botanical:
 Calendula leaves,
 ¹/₂ cup ground
Cooling rack
Cutting board
Disposable chopstick,
 bamboo
Distilled water
Fats:
 Coconut oil
 Olive oil
 Palm oil
 Sunflower oil
Glass juice jar
 with lid, 48 oz.
Hammer
Kitchen knife,
 sharp unserrated
Laboratory
 thermometer (with
 stainless steel shaft),
 0° to 180° F

Large nail
Latex gloves
Lye crystals
Masking tape
Measuring cup
 with pouring spout
Mold:
 Plastic or wooden
 container with lid
Plastic garbage bag
Protective eyewear
Scale (must be able to
 weigh up to 5 lb.)
Scented oils:
 Lavender essential, 1 tsp.
 Mango fragrance, 2 tsp.
 Tangerine essential, 3 tsp.
Stainless steel
 stockpot, 12 qt.
Wooden spoon

One Batch of Cold-process Soap Recipe

Distilled water, 32 oz.
Fats:
 Coconut oil, 30 oz.
 Olive oil, 14 oz.
 Palm oil, 24 oz.
 Sunflower oil, 18 oz.

Lye crystals, 12 oz.
Mold: 11" long x
 9" wide x 3" deep

*Refer to Note
on page 55.*

How do I substitute exotic fats for basic fats when making cold-process soap?

The basic fats used in the cold-process method of making soap include coconut oil, olive oil, palm oil, and/or vegetable shortening. Each of these fats has unique benefits including skin conditioning and good latherability. In addition, a nice hard bar of soap that will last longer than other soaps is produced. In this case, other fats have been included for added skin conditioning benefits.

Rosebud/Sandalwood/Vanilla Cold-process Soap Bars

Here's How:

1. Refer back to Technique 15: Steps 1–19 on pages 57–59, using the recipe at right.

9
project

What You Need To Get Started:

Bath towels
Blanket
Cooling rack
Cutting board
Disposable chopstick,
  bamboo
Distilled water
Fats:
  Almond oil
  Apricot kernel oil
  Coconut oil
  Jojoba oil
  Olive oil
  Palm oil
  Shea butter
Glass juice jar
  with lid, 48 oz.
Hammer
Kitchen knife,
  sharp unserrated
Laboratory
  thermometer (with
  stainless steel shaft),
  0° to 180° F

Large nail
Latex gloves
Lye crystals
Masking tape
Measuring cup
  with pouring spout
Mold:
  Plastic or wooden
  container with lid
Plastic garbage bag
Protective eyewear
Scale (must be able to
  weigh up to 5 lb.)
Scented oils:
  Rosebud fragrance, 2 tsp.
  Sandalwood essential, 1 tsp.
  Vanilla fragrance, 5 tsp.
Stainless steel
  stockpot, 12 qt.
Wooden spoon

One Batch of Cold-process Soap Recipe

Distilled water, 31 oz.
Fats:
  Almond oil, 5 oz.
  Apricot kernel oil,
    5 oz.
  Coconut oil, 36 oz.
  Jojoba oil, 2 oz.
  Olive oil, 14 oz.

Palm oil, 18 oz.
Shea butter, 2 oz.
Lye crystals, 12 oz.
Mold: 11" long x
  9" wide x 3" deep

*Refer to Note
on page 55.*

How do I make other personal care items?

Salt glow, bath salts, and massage oils, scented to match a favorite glycerin melt-and-pour, rebatched, or cold-process soap, complement one another. When placed in carefully selected bottles and jars, the perfect gift set is created.

Salt Glow

Here's How:

1. Place sea salt, grapeseed oil, and scented oils in a wide-mouth jar and mix well. Place a scalloped shell on top of the mixture. This shell will be used to scoop the salt glow out of the jar when ready to use. Place the lid on the jar.

2. To use the salt glow, scoop an appropriate amount out of the jar. Gently rub the salt glow over areas of the body to remove dry skin. Thoroughly rinse salt glow off with running water.

Bath Salts

Here's How:

1. Place epsom, ice cream rock, and sea salts in mixing bowl and mix well.

2. Add glycerin, liquid colorants, and scented oils.

Gently stir to evenly distribute the color.

3. Spoon the mixture into a wide-mouth jar and place a scalloped shell on top of the mixture. This shell will be used to scoop the bath salt out of the jar when ready to use. Place the lid on the jar.

4. To use the bath salts, place three to five scoops under running water.

Massage Oil

Here's How:

1. Place oils and liquid Vitamin E in bottle and mix well.

2. Place assorted shells in bottle.

3. To use the massage oil, place a small amount into the palm of your hand and use for massage.

What You Need To Get Started:

Salt Glow:
Grapeseed oil, $^1/_4$ cup
Scented oils:
  Rosewood essential, $^1/_4$ tsp.
  Sandalwood essential, $^1/_4$ tsp.
  Vanilla fragrance, $^1/_2$ tsp.
Sea salt, 1 cup
Shell, scalloped
Wide-mouth jar with lid, 32 oz.

Bath Salts:
Epsom salt, $^3/_4$ cup
Glycerin, 1 tbsp.
Ice cream rock salt, $1^1/_2$ cups
Liquid colorants:
  Blue, 2 drops
  Orange, 8 drops
  Red, 1 drop
Mixing bowl
Scented oils:
  Rosewood essential, $^1/_4$ tsp.
  Sandalwood essential, $^1/_4$ tsp.
  Vanilla fragrance, $^1/_2$ tsp.
Sea salt, $^3/_4$ cup
Shell, scalloped
Wide-mouth jar with lid, 48 oz.

Massage Oil:
Almond oil, $^3/_4$ cup
Bottle with sealing lid
  or cork, 12 oz.
Grapeseed oil, $^3/_4$ cup
Liquid Vitamin E, 6 drops
Scented oils:
  Rosewood essential, $^3/_8$ tsp.
  Sandalwood essential, $^3/_8$ tsp.
  Vanilla fragrance, $^3/_4$ tsp.
Shells, assorted small

Section 4:
gallery

Created by Libby Claridge, Earth Dance

Libby Claridge established her company, Earth Dance, in 1996 as a result of an ever increasing desire to create something beautiful, to be her own boss, and to help spread environmental awareness.

Her business has grown into a small full-time business with accounts throughout the United States and Canada. Utilizing her degree in biology, she moves her product out of the realm of merely mixing ingredients together into an understanding of the science of soapmaking. Because she feels that her soaps should encompass a total sensory experience, producing a bar that is aesthetically pleasing is just as important as the ingredients that go into it.

Libby feels that her soaps should emulate Mother Nature in her grace and beauty. Her soaps convey the rich hues of the earth by using clays, herbs, and flowers. The aromas encompass the subtle to the exotic with essential oils of patchouli, lavender, and lemongrass. Rich, skin-loving oils and butters are always added to her soap recipes.

appointed her with bulky shapes, poor designs, fragrances, or packaging. One day, after chasing a huge slab of colorful soap in the bathtub, only to have it fall apart in her hands, she decided there had to be a better way to make glycerin soap.

Joanna embraced her new creative challenge with enthusiasm and confidence. Over a year of intense research and experimentation with dozens of glycerin soap bases, ingredient variations, fragrances, and techniques led her to the answers and results she was looking for.

With the feedback and support of friends and family, Joanna incorporated her soap designs into six different collections. Her meticulously handcrafted soaps have an aura of glamour with a whimsical twist, by combining intriguing and inspiring fragrances with vibrant colors, fun shapes, and sleek packaging.

As her company is growing, Joanna loves being actively involved in every aspect of her business. When she's out of the office, Joanna spends most of her time with family and is a passionate animal lover, which explains the number of family companions—seven cats and a feisty dog.

Her hopes and expectations for the future are simple: to maintain the joy of creating something special and to treat the environment and its divers inhabitants with unequivocal respect, while continuing to supply high-quality products with integrity and innovation.

Joanna Langada-Korn, founder of KoolSoap™, began soap crafting in early 1998. The popularity of glycerin soaps in recent years had caught her attention as a consumer and she was immediately attracted to the novelty of these creations. She soon discovered that most brands had left the "good-for-your-skin" glycerin buried in a long list of undesirable ingredients, while the handmade varieties dis-

Created by Joanna Langada-Korn, KoolSoap™

Created by Joanna Langada-Korn, KoolSoap™

Marie Browning is a consummate craft designer, making a career of designing products, writing books and articles, plus teaching and demonstrating.

You may have already enjoyed her popular soapmaking books entitled, *Beautiful Handmade Natural Soaps* and *Melt & Pour Soapmaking.* In addition to soapmaking, Marie has authored several other books, *Handcrafted Journals, Albums, Scrapbooks & More, Gifts From Your Garden, Memory Gifts, Hand Decorated Paper,* and *Parchment Art.* Her articles and designs have appeared in *Handcraft Illustrated, Better Homes & Gardens, Canadian Stamper, Great American Craft, All American Crafts,* and in numerous project books.

Marie has also made television appearances on the Sue Warden Show in Canada.

As a consultant for a melt-and-pour manufacturer, she was instrumental in their fragrance crafting product development and has written two soapmaking books for them: *Handmade Designer Soaps* and *The Art of Fragrance Crafting.*

Marie earned a fine arts diploma from Camosun College and attended the University of Victoria. She is a certified professional demonstrator, a professional affiliate of the Canadian Craft and Hobby Association, and a member of the Stencil Artisan's League and the Society of Craft Designers.

Marie Browning lives, gardens, and crafts on Vancouver Island in Canada. She and her husband Scott have three children: Katelyn, Lena, and Jonathan.

Created by Marie Browning

Created by Airyana Markham, Nile Botanical

Airyana Markham, owner of Nile Botanical, established her business in 1997. The business evolved out of a love and interest for hand-made natural products—especially those recipes and procedures that have been handed down from one generation or culture to another.

Egyptians love things that are aesthetically pleasing to the senses—the inspiration for the products they produce. The whimsical version of the white chocolate raspberry cheesecake soap is not only made from natural ingredients, but is a lot of fun to the senses too!

Airyana has gone back to the basics and has found luxury there.

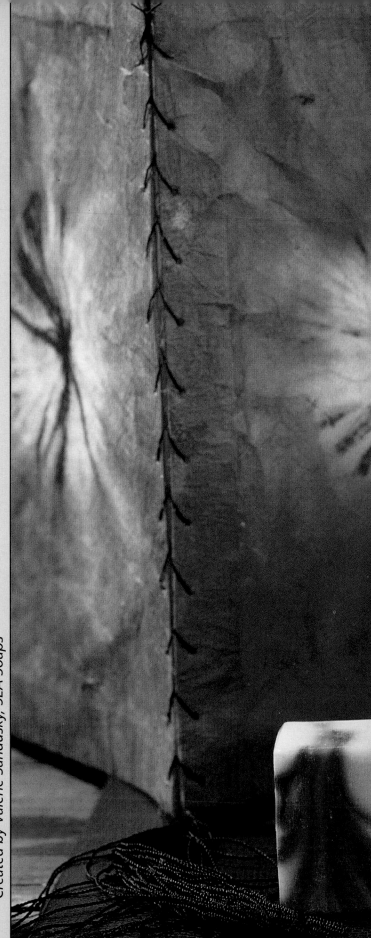

Valerie Sandusky, owner of SEA Soaps, began making soap as a hobbyist back in 1990 after reading an article about a couple making soaps to sell at a farmer's market. As a lifelong crafter, the thought of soapmaking intrigued Valerie. She mail-ordered the only two books she could find on the subject and read them cover to cover the day they arrived. After purchasing the needed supplies, within a week she had made her first batch of soap. She continued making soap for personal use and to give as gifts to friends and relatives. However, soapmaking soon became an addiction and she began selling her handcrafted soap part-time while holding down a full-time job. Soon her love for soapmaking outweighed her love for other crafts and they began to fall by the wayside.

In 1995 Valerie decided it was time to take the small, but steadily growing business to a higher level. She quit her full-time job and moved her soapmaking out of her kitchen and into a small trailer located on her property. Soon she began wholesaling her soaps to retail stores.

Valerie's soapmaking skills have come a long way since she stirred up that first batch. She now regularly makes 36 different varieties incorporating various pigments, dyes, essential oils, fragrance oils, and botanicals to make each batch unique. SEA Soaps can be found coast to coast in various retail stores, including her own retail outlet store in Ketchikan, Alaska.

Created by Valerie Sandusky, SEA Soaps

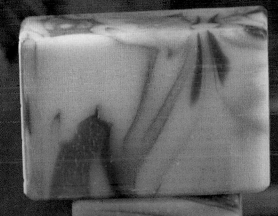

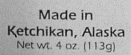

SEA Soaps

Pure Handcrafted Soap
With Olive Oil

Made in
Ketchikan, Alaska
Net wt. 4 oz. (113g)

Kathy Wawrzyniak, "The Soap Lady," lives in Sandy, Utah. She is the mother of four wonderful sons, and the grandmother of two "perfect" grandchildren!

Kathy has been handcrafting vegetable glycerin soap for four years. She enjoys this process because she feels it lends itself so well to pigment and fragrance—the pigment stays bright and strong and the fragrance remains true.

Handcrafting soap has become a family adventure—sons and daughters-in-law join in creating and handcrafting her soap. It is so rewarding to feel the anticipation of the whole family when a new loaf of soap is "ready to be born." Even more so when she witnesses people admiring her soaps and the realization that these creations bring pleasure to many.

Created by Kathy Wawrzyniak, "The Soap Lady"

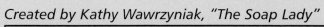
Created by Kathy Wawrzyniak, "The Soap Lady"

Created by Kathy Wawrzyniak, "The Soap Lady"

C. Kaila Westerman is an avid soap and candle crafter and owner of a mail-order craft supply company, TKB Trading. She has served as a speaker at the Hand-crafted Soap Maker's Guild gatherings and her articles have appeared in *The Soapmaker's Newsletter, By Hand, Creative Alchemy,* and *The Saponifier.* She also has an educational website that offers soap recipes and ideas.

Kaila recently published a book on soap crafting, *Melt and Mold Soapcrafting,* and is currently working on a manuscript for gel candle crafting.

She lives in Oakland, California, with her husband of 15 years.

Created by C. Kaila Westerman, TKB Trading

Created by C. Kaila Westerman, TKB Trading

Acknowledgments

We would like to thank the following companies for providing materials used in this publication.

Browning, Marie
7069 Silverdale Place
Brentwood Bay, BC Canada
Phone: (250) 652-7057
Website: www.mariebrowning.com

Delta Technical Coatings
2550 Pellissier Place
Whittier, CA 90601
Phone: (800) 423-4135
Website: www.deltacrafts.com
Melt-and-pour soap base, liquid colorants, molds, scented oils, and metallic and iridescent powders

Earth Dance (Libby Claridge)
P.O. Box 2101
Julian, CA 92036
Phone: (760) 765-2171
Website: www.earthdancesoaps.com

Fields Landing Soap Factory
South Bay Depot Road
Fields Landing, CA 95537-0365
Phone: (707) 443-9323
Website: www.eti-usa.com
Melt-and-pour soap base, liquid and solid colorants, liquid soap, molds, and scented oils

KoolSoap™ (Joanna Langada-Korn)
P.O. Box 1043
Carmel, NY 10512
Phone: (845) 225-7424
Website: www.koolsoap.com

Life of the Party
832 Ridgewood Avenue, Bldg. #2
North Brunswick, NJ 08902
Phone: (732) 828-0886
Melt-and-pour soap base, liquid colorants, molds, loaf soap, and molded soap inserts and curls

Milky Way Molds
PMB 473
Portland, OR 97206
Phone: (800) 588-7930
Website: www.milkywaysoapmolds.com
Soap stamps and molds

Nile Botanical (Airyana Markham)
Salt Lake City, UT
E-mail: nilebotanical@aol.com

SEA Soaps (Valerie Sandusky)
P.O. Box 5865
Ketchikan, AK 99901
Phone: (907) 247-6277
Website: www.seasoaps.com

Soapcrafters
2944 S. West Temple
Salt Lake City, UT 84115
Phone: (801) 484-5121
Website: www.soapcrafters.com
Melt-and-pour soap base, liquid colorants, molds, scented oils, botanicals, and grated soap for rebatching

Soapsations by Yaley Enterprises
7664 Avianca Drive
Redding, CA 96002
Phone: (530) 365-5252
Website: www.yaley.com
Frosting soap, liquid colorants, and scented oils

"The Soap Lady" (Kathy Wawrzyniak)
9875 Kramer Drive
Sandy, UT 84092
Phone: (801) 651-6051
E-mail: comeofage@earthlink.net

TKB Trading (C. Kaila Westerman)
356 24th Street
Oakland, CA 94612
Phone: (510) 451-9011
Website: www.tkbtrading.com
Website: www.alphabetsoap.com

Metric conversions

INCHES TO MILLIMETRES AND CENTIMETRES

MM-Millimetres   CM-Centimetres

INCHES	MM	CM	INCHES	CM	INCHES	CM
$\frac{1}{8}$	3	0.9	9	22.9	30	76.2
$\frac{1}{4}$	6	0.6	10	25.4	31	78.7
$\frac{3}{8}$	10	1.0	11	27.9	32	81.3
$\frac{1}{2}$	13	1.3	12	30.5	33	83.8
$\frac{5}{8}$	16	1.6	13	33.0	34	86.4
$\frac{3}{4}$	19	1.9	14	35.6	35	88.9
$\frac{7}{8}$	22	2.2	15	38.1	36	91.4
1	25	2.5	16	40.6	37	94.0
$1\frac{1}{4}$	32	3.2	17	43.2	38	96.5
$1\frac{1}{2}$	38	3.8	18	45.7	39	99.1
$1\frac{3}{4}$	44	4.4	19	48.3	40	101.6
2	51	5.1	20	50.8	41	104.1
$2\frac{1}{2}$	64	6.4	21	53.3	42	106.7
3	76	7.6	22	55.9	43	109.2
$3\frac{1}{2}$	89	8.9	23	58.4	44	111.8
4	102	10.2	24	61.0	45	114.3
$4\frac{1}{2}$	114	11.4	25	63.5	46	116.8
5	127	12.7	26	66.0	47	119.4
6	152	15.2	27	68.6	48	121.9
7	178	17.8	28	71.1	49	124.5
8	203	20.3	29	73.7	50	127.0

YARDS TO METRES

YARDS	METRES	YARDS	METRES	YARDS	METRES	YARDS	METRES	YARDS	METRES
$\frac{1}{8}$	0.11	$2\frac{1}{8}$	1.94	$4\frac{1}{8}$	3.77	$6\frac{1}{8}$	5.60	$8\frac{1}{8}$	7.43
$\frac{1}{4}$	0.23	$2\frac{1}{4}$	2.06	$4\frac{1}{4}$	3.89	$6\frac{1}{4}$	5.72	$8\frac{1}{4}$	7.54
$\frac{3}{8}$	0.34	$2\frac{3}{8}$	2.17	$4\frac{3}{8}$	4.00	$6\frac{3}{8}$	5.83	$8\frac{3}{8}$	7.66
$\frac{1}{2}$	0.46	$2\frac{1}{2}$	2.29	$4\frac{1}{2}$	4.11	$6\frac{1}{2}$	5.94	$8\frac{1}{2}$	7.77
$\frac{5}{8}$	0.57	$2\frac{5}{8}$	2.40	$4\frac{5}{8}$	4.23	$6\frac{5}{8}$	6.06	$8\frac{5}{8}$	7.89
$\frac{3}{4}$	0.69	$2\frac{3}{4}$	2.51	$4\frac{3}{4}$	4.34	$6\frac{3}{4}$	6.17	$8\frac{3}{4}$	8.00
$\frac{7}{8}$	0.80	$2\frac{7}{8}$	2.63	$4\frac{7}{8}$	4.46	$6\frac{7}{8}$	6.29	$8\frac{7}{8}$	8.12
1	0.91	3	2.74	5	4.57	7	6.40	9	8.23
$1\frac{1}{8}$	1.03	$3\frac{1}{8}$	2.86	$5\frac{1}{8}$	4.69	$7\frac{1}{8}$	6.52	$9\frac{1}{8}$	8.34
$1\frac{1}{4}$	1.14	$3\frac{1}{4}$	2.97	$5\frac{1}{4}$	4.80	$7\frac{1}{4}$	6.63	$9\frac{1}{4}$	8.46
$1\frac{3}{8}$	1.26	$3\frac{3}{8}$	3.09	$5\frac{3}{8}$	4.91	$7\frac{3}{8}$	6.74	$9\frac{3}{8}$	8.57
$1\frac{1}{2}$	1.37	$3\frac{1}{2}$	3.20	$5\frac{1}{2}$	5.03	$7\frac{1}{2}$	6.86	$9\frac{1}{2}$	8.69
$1\frac{5}{8}$	1.49	$3\frac{5}{8}$	3.31	$5\frac{5}{8}$	5.14	$7\frac{5}{8}$	6.97	$9\frac{5}{8}$	8.80
$1\frac{3}{4}$	1.60	$3\frac{3}{4}$	3.43	$5\frac{3}{4}$	5.26	$7\frac{3}{4}$	7.09	$9\frac{3}{4}$	8.92
$1\frac{7}{8}$	1.71	$3\frac{7}{8}$	3.54	$5\frac{7}{8}$	5.37	$7\frac{7}{8}$	7.20	$9\frac{7}{8}$	9.03
2	1.83	4	3.66	6	5.49	8	7.32	10	9.14

Index